LANGUAGE ARTS
INSTANT ASSESSMENTS
for Data Tracking
Kindergarten

Credits
Content Editor: Jennifer B. Stith

Visit *carsondellosa.com* for correlations to Common Core, state, national, and Canadian provincial standards.

Carson-Dellosa Publishing, LLC
PO Box 35665
Greensboro, NC 27425 USA
carsondellosa.com

978-1-4838-3615-7
01-339161151

Table of Contents

✦ Assessment and Data Tracking ✦

Data tracking is an essential element in modern classrooms. Teachers are often required to capture student learning through both formative and summative assessments. They then must use the results to guide teaching, remediation, and lesson planning and provide feedback to students, parents, and administrators. Because time is always at a premium in the classroom, it is vital that teachers have the assessments they need at their fingertips. The assessments need to be suited to the skill being assessed as well as adapted to the stage in the learning process. This is true for an informal checkup at the end of a lesson or a formal assessment at the end of a unit.

This book will provide the tools and assessments needed to determine your students' level of mastery throughout the school year. The assessments are both formal and informal and include a variety of formats—pretests and posttests, flash cards, prompt cards, traditional tests, and exit tickets. Often, there are several assessment options for a single skill or concept to allow you the greatest flexibility when assessing understanding. Simply select the assessment that best fits your needs, or use them all to create a comprehensive set of assessments for before, during, and after learning.

Incorporate Instant Assessments into your daily plans to streamline the data-tracking process and keep the focus on student mastery and growth.

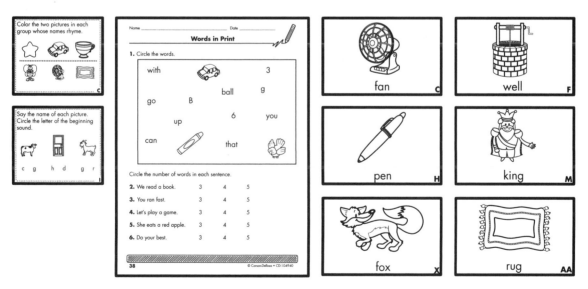

A variety of instant assessments for foundational skills

Types of Assessment

Assessment usually has a negative association because it brings to mind tedious pencil-and-paper tests and grading. However, it can take on many different forms and be a positive, integral part of the year. Not all assessments need to be formal, nor do they all need to be graded. Choose the type of assessment to use based on the information you need to gather. Then, you can decide if or how it should be graded.

	What Does It Look Like?	Examples
Formative Assessment	• occurs during learning • is administered frequently • is usually informal and not graded • identifies areas of improvement • provides immediate feedback so a student can make adjustments promptly, if needed • allows teachers to rethink strategies, lesson content, etc., based on current student performance • is process-focused • has the most impact on a student's performance	• in-class observations • exit tickets • reflections and journaling • homework • student-teacher conferences • student self-evaluations
Interim Assessment	• occurs occasionally • is more formal and usually graded • feedback is not immediate, though still fairly quick • helps teachers identify gaps in teaching and areas for remediation • often includes performance assessments, which are individualized, authentic, and performance-based in order to evaluate higher-level thinking skills	• in-class observations • exit tickets • reflections and journaling • homework • student-teacher conferences • student self-evaluations
Summative Assessment	• occurs once learning is considered complete • the information is used by the teacher and school for broader purposes • takes time to return a grade or score • can be used to compare a student's performance to others • is product-focused • has the least impact on a student's performance since there are few or no opportunities for retesting	• cumulative projects • final portfolios • quarterly testing • end-of-the-year testing • standardized testing

How to Use This Book

The assessments in this book follow a few different formats, depending on the skill or concept being assessed. Use the descriptions below to familiarize yourself with each unique format and get the most out of Instant Assessments all year long.

Show What You Know

Most anchors begin with two *Show What You Know* tests. They follow the same format with the same types of questions, so they can be used as a pretest and posttest that can be directly compared to show growth. Or, use one as a test at the end of a unit and use the second version as a retest for students after remediation.

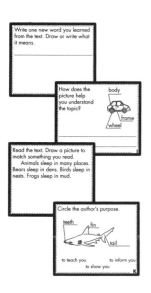

Exit Tickets

Most anchors end with exit tickets that cover the variety of concepts within the anchor. Exit tickets are very targeted questions designed to assess understanding of specific skills, so they are ideal formative assessments to use at the end of a lesson. Exit tickets do not have space for student names, allowing teachers to gather information on the entire class without placing pressure on individual students. If desired, have students write their names or initials on the back of the tickets. Other uses for exit tickets include the following:

- Use the back of each ticket for longer answers, fuller explanations, or extension questions. If needed, students can staple them to larger sheets of paper.
- They can also be used for warm-ups or to find out what students know before a lesson.
- Use the generic exit tickets on pages 7 and 8 for any concept you want to assess. Be sure to fill in any blanks before copying.
- Laminate them and place them in a language arts center as task cards.
- Use them to play Scoot or a similar review game at the end of a unit.
- Choose several to create a targeted assessment for a skill or set of skills.

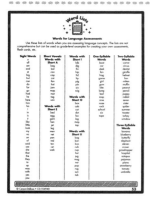

Word Lists

Word lists consist of several collections of grade-appropriate words in areas that students need to be assessed in, such as sight words, spelling patterns, and words with affixes. They are not comprehensive but are intended to make creating your own assessments simpler. Use the word lists to create vocabulary tests, word decoding fluency tests, spelling lists, etc., for the year.

Cards

Use the cards as prompts for one-on-one conferencing. Simply copy the cards, cut them apart, and follow the directions preceding each set of cards. Use the lettering to keep track of which cards a student has interacted with.

- Copy on card stock and/or laminate for durability.
- Punch holes in the top left corners and place the cards on a book ring to make them easily accessible.
- Copy the sets on different colors of paper to keep them easily separated or to distinguish different sections within a set of cards.
- Easily differentiate by using different amounts or levels of cards to assess a student.
- Write the answers on the backs of cards to create self-checking flash cards.
- Place them in a language arts center as task cards or matching activities.
- Use them to play Scoot or a similar review game at the end of a unit.

Assessment Pages

The reproducible assessment pages are intended for use as a standard test of a skill. Use them in conjunction with other types of assessment to get a full picture of a student's level of understanding. They can also be used for review or homework.

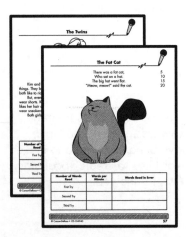

Fluency Pages

Use the paired fluency pages to assess students' oral reading fluency. Provide a copy of the student page to the student, and use the teacher copy to track how far the student read, which words he or she struggled with, and the student's performance on repeated readings. The word count is provided at the end of each line for easy totaling. Then, use the related comprehension questions to assess the student's understanding of what he or she read.

Exit Tickets

Exit tickets are a useful formative assessment tool that you can easily work into your day. You can choose to use a single exit ticket at the end of the day or at the end of each lesson. Simply choose a ticket below and make one copy for each student. Then, have students complete the prompt and present them to you as their ticket out of the door. Use the student responses to gauge overall learning, create small remediation groups, or target areas for reteaching. A blank exit ticket is included on page 8 so you can create your own exit tickets as well.

What stuck with you today?

_____

_____

_____

List three facts you learned today. Put them in order from most important to least important.

1. _____

2. _____

3. _____

The first thing I'll tell my family about today is

_____

_____

_____.

The most important thing I learned today is

_____

_____

_____.

Color the face that shows how you feel about understanding today's lesson.

Explain why. _____

Summarize today's lesson in 10 words or less.

_____

_____

_____

One example of _____ is _____

_____

_____

_____ .

One question I still have is _____

_____

_____

_____ .

How will understanding _____

_____

help you in real life? _____

_____

_____

One new word I learned today is

_____ .

It means _____

_____

_____ .

Draw a picture related to the lesson. Add a caption.

_____

_____

If today's lesson were a song, the title would be _____

_____

because _____

_____ .

The answer is _____ .

What is the question? _____

_____

_____

_____

✦ Show What You Know ✦
Reading: Literature

Read the story. Circle the answers.

Friends are **special**. Lynn and Rose are friends. They ride the bus to school. They help each other read. They go places together. They are happy to be friends.

1. What is the story about?

      toys   friends   books

2. Which word describes friends?

      sad   read   special

3. How do the girls feel about being friends?

      happy   sad   angry

4. What do the girls ride to school?

      car   train   bus

Name _____ Date _____

✦ Show What You Know ✦
Reading: Literature

Read the poem. Circle the answers.

Little boy blue,
Come blow your horn,
The sheep's in the **meadow**,
The cow's in the corn.
Where is the boy
Who looks after the sheep?
He's under a haystack
Fast asleep.

1. Who looks after the sheep?

farmer   boy   cow

2. What is the boy doing instead?

singing   eating   sleeping

3. What helps you understand the meaning of the word **meadow**?

text   picture

4. Why type of text is this?

poem   story

Key Details

Read the story. Circle the answers.

Mom told Andy it was time to go shopping. Andy put on his shoes and coat. They got in the car. Mom drove to the grocery store. Mom parked the car in the lot. They got a cart. Andy was excited! Mom let Andy choose a snack for his lunch. Their cart was full. They paid. It was time to drive home.

1. Who was in the car?

Andy   Beth   Mom

2. Where did Mom take Andy?

park   school   store

3. How does Andy feel?

sad   excited   angry

4. What did Andy get to choose at the store?

snack   bread   plate

Beginning, Middle, and End

Read the story. Draw a picture to show what happened in the beginning, middle, and end of the story.

   Kate is having a party. She hangs balloons. She puts out food to eat. Her friends are here! They dance. They play games. Then, they eat pizza and cake. Kate loves to have a party!

Beginning

Middle

End

Characters and Settings

Use the cards to assess students' understanding of characters and settings. Have students look at the cards and tell what they see. Have them sort the cards by characters or settings. Alternatively, have students choose one character and one setting. Have them tell a story using the two cards as a beginning.

G

H

I

J

K

L

M

N

Characters and Settings

This is a picture from a story. Circle the answers to the questions.

1. What is the setting of the story?

house   pond   forest

2. Who are the characters in the story?

boy   bear   man   dog

3. Which sentences could be part of this story?

It was a sunny day.

It was a rainy day.

The boy caught a big fish.

The dog caught a frog.

Types of Text

Look at each text. Circle the type of text.

1.

Roses are red,

Violets are blue,

Sugar is sweet,

And so are you.

story   **poem**

2. Miguel looked out the window. He
saw Earth behind him. It looked
very small. Then, he looked at
Pluto. That is where he is going. He
will like his new home.

story   **poem**

3. What is one difference between a story and a poem?

_____

_____

Illustrations

1. Circle the picture that gives you clues about what the boy is making.

2. Circle the picture that gives you clues about what animal the girl is feeding.

3. Circle the picture that gives you clues about what plant will grow.

Comparing and Contrasting
Characters and Settings

Think about the stories *Goldilocks and the Three Bears* and *Little Red Riding Hood*. Use the word bank to help you write or draw about the things that are the same and different in the two stories.

basket	bed	brave	chair	curious
Grandma	helpful	little girl	porridge	sleepy
	three bears	wolf	woods	

Goldilocks and the Three Bears	Both	*Little Red Riding Hood*

Draw or write two details from the story.

A

Write a new title for the story.

_____

_____

_____

_____

_____

B

Draw or write something that happens in the beginning, middle, and end of the story.

Beginning	Middle	End

C

Draw a picture of the character at the beginning of the story.

D

Draw a picture of the character at the end of the story.

E

Draw a setting for this boy.

F

Draw one event from the story.

G

Look at the pictures. Draw what happens next.

H

A poem is

_____

_____

_____

_____

_____ .

I

A story is

_____

_____

_____

_____

_____ .

J

Read the story. Circle the objects in Belle's backpack.

Belle has a new backpack. It is red. She puts a box of crayons in her backpack. She puts in some pencils. Now, she is ready for school!

crayons

K

Compare and contrast two characters. Draw or write details in the diagram.

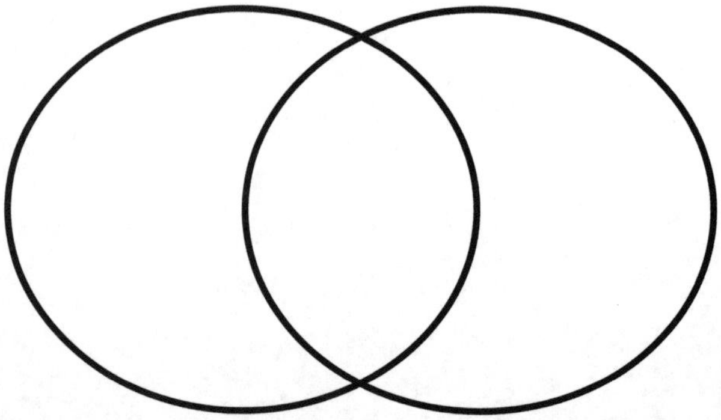

L

Name _____   Date _____

Read the text. Circle the answers.

Tigers are the biggest wildcats in the world! They have orange and white fur. They have black stripes. Tigers hunt for food. They hunt at night. They use their big claws. They can eat a lot of meat! Tigers are great swimmers. They like to cool off in the water.

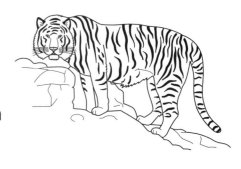

Tigers are **endangered**. This means that they are hunted too much. Now, tigers are being helped. Save the tigers!

1. What shows you how a tiger looks?

       picture   text

2. What tells how a tiger looks?

       picture   text

3. How do tigers get food?

      growl   hunt   sleep

4. Which words tell the meaning of the word **endangered**?

    hunted too much   great swimmers

5. Why did the author write this text?

    to teach you about tigers   to make you laugh

Name _____   Date _____

Read the text. Circle the answers.

A snake is a **reptile**. A reptile is a cold-blooded animal. It has scales. Scales look like tiny squares or diamonds. They are hard. They cover a snake's body. Snakes can grow long.

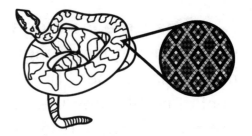

Snakes live all over the world. They can live in deserts or in rain forests.

1. What is a **reptile**?

a warm-blooded animal   a cold-blooded animal

2. What covers a snake's body?

fur   scales   feathers

3. What shape are scales?

   ◯   ◇

4. Where is one place the text says snakes can live?

rain forests   ice   ocean

5. Why did the illustrator draw an up-close view of a snake's skin?

so that you can see the scales

so that you know where snakes live

Name _____ Date _____

Key Details

Read the text. Circle the answers.

Pandas live in forests. The forests are in China. They have black and white fur. Pandas are good climbers. Pandas eat bamboo. They eat fast. They eat a lot. Pandas are good tree climbers.

1. Where do pandas live?

in water   in forests   under the ground

2. What two colors is a panda?

red and blue   brown and blue   black and white

3. What do pandas eat?

bamboo   corn   bugs

4. What do pandas climb?

walls   trees   cars

Name _____ Date _____

Main Idea

Read the text. Circle the answers.

Every animal has a home. Animals make their homes in different places. Birds make nests in trees. Bees make hives in trees. Ants make homes under the ground. Bats live in caves.

1. What is the main idea of this text?

Animals have homes.   Animals live in caves.

2. Some animals build homes in _____.

trees   trucks   boxes

3. Some animals have homes under the _____.

apples   ground   street

4. Other animals have homes in _____.

caves   cones   wheels

Name _____ Date _____

Comparing and Contrasting Two Ideas

Read each sentence. Decide if the information is the same or different. Draw an **X** in the correct column.

	Same	Different
1. Dogs and cats are animals.		
2. Dogs bark. Cats meow.		
3. Dogs and cats have four feet.		
4. Baby cats are called kittens. Baby dogs are called puppies.		
5. Dogs and cats can be good pets.		
6. Dogs and cats have fur.		
7. Cats purr. Dogs bark.		

8.　　　Draw a picture of a cat.　　　　Draw a picture of a dog.

Learning New Words

Read the text. Circle the answers.

An apple is a fruit. The **skin** of an apple can be red, yellow, or green. The juicy part of an apple is the **flesh**. The middle of the apple is called the **core**. You do not eat the core. An apple's **seeds** are in the core.

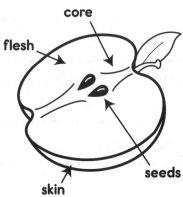

1. Which word means the outside of an apple?

skin   flesh   core

2. Which word means the juicy part of an apple?

seeds   core   flesh

3. Circle the seeds in the picture.

4. Color the apple's core green.

Parts of a Book

Draw lines to connect each label to the correct book part.

front cover

This is the story
of a very nice
bear and
his toys.

back cover

The Best Toys

by T. D. Bear

Illustrations by
Dolly Wolly

title page

The Best Toys

spine

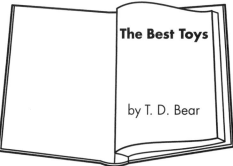

The Best Toys

by T. D. Bear

Finding the Parts of a Book

Find three books in your classroom or library. Look at the front cover of each book. Then, complete the chart.

1. What is the name of the book? Write the book's **title**.	2. Who wrote the book? Write the name of the **author**.	3. Who drew the pictures? Write the name of the **illustrator**.
_____ _____	_____ _____	_____ _____
_____ _____	_____ _____	_____ _____
_____ _____	_____ _____	_____ _____

Name _____ Date _____

Author and Illustrator

Look at the picture of a book. Follow the directions.

All About Birds

by Sally Nest

Illustrations by
Bob Branch

1. Use a red crayon to circle the author's name.

2. Use a blue crayon to circle the illustrator's name.

Circle the answers. Write the answers on the lines.

3. An author _____.

draws pictures   writes words

4. An illustrator _____.

draws pictures   writes words

Illustrations and Text

Read the text. Draw lines to connect each word to the body part it names.

Your body has many parts. You have two arms with hands. You have two legs with feet. Your head is on top of your body. It has eyes, a nose, a mouth, and ears.

head

eye

nose

ear

mouth

arm

hand

leg

foot

Author's Purpose

Read the text. Circle the answers. Write the answers on the lines.

Fluffy is missing!
Fluffy is a cat with orange spots. She has yellow eyes. Fluffy has a blue collar. Please call Kit at 555-2134 if you see Fluffy. Thank you!

1. The author of this poster is

_____ .

Kit   Fluffy

2. She wrote the poster because

_____ .

her dog is lost   her cat is lost

3. What word from the poster is a clue as to why the author wrote this?

_____ .

Read the text. Answer the questions.

I am big and furry, and I live in a cave. I like to sleep all winter long. I also like to eat honey! What am I?

4. An author wrote this _____ .

poem   riddle

5. He wrote this to _____ .

entertain you   inform you

Comparing and Contrasting Texts

Read the texts. Follow the directions.

Ty likes to watch clouds. He likes puffy clouds. He thinks they look like cotton balls. He once saw a cloud that looked like an airplane. Clouds can look like many things.

Some clouds are white. Some are dark. Dark clouds mean a storm is coming. Clouds are made of water. Rain falls from clouds.

1. Circle the text that tells you facts about clouds.

2. Draw a green dot next to the text that tells how a boy thinks clouds look.

3. Draw a red **X** next the text that tells about colors of clouds.

4. Draw a blue dot next to the text that tells a story.

Write two facts you learned from the text.

_____

_____

_____

_____

A

Draw picture of one detail in the text.

B

What is the main idea of the text?

_____

_____

_____

_____

_____

C

Draw or write how the texts are the same and different.

D

Write one new word you learned from the text. Draw or write what it means.

_____

E

Write one new word you learned from the text. Write the words from the text that helped you understand the new word.

_____

_____

_____

F

Where do you find the title of a book? Circle your answer.

title page

last page

G

Find a book. Write the author's name. Write the illustrator's name.

_____

_____

_____

_____

H

How does the picture help you understand the topic?

body

frame

wheel

_____

_____

I

Read the text. Draw a picture to match something you read.

    Animals sleep in many places. Bears sleep in dens. Birds sleep in nests. Frogs sleep in mud.

J

Circle the author's purpose.

gills

fin

tail

to teach you   to inform you

to show you

K

Choose two books on the same topic. Draw or write two things you learned from each book that are different.

L

Name _____ Date _____

✦ Show What You Know ✦
Reading: Foundational Skills

1. Circle the words in each sentence. Then, circle the number of words.

My dog has a blue collar.   4   5   6

His name is Woofy.   4   5   6

2. Match the uppercase and lowercase letters.

H	x
L	h
B	d
X	l
D	b

3. Say the name of each picture. Circle the pictures whose names rhyme.

4. Say the name of each picture. Circle the number of syllables.

1   2   3   1   2   3   1   2   3   1   2   3

5. Say the name of each picture. Color only the letters whose sounds you hear in each word.

   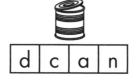   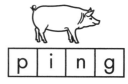

w	t	e	b

d	c	a	n

p	i	n	g

6. Read each word. Change one letter to spell the name of the picture.

ten   _____   pan   _____

✦ Show What You Know
Reading: Foundational Skills

1. Circle the words in each sentence. Then, circle the number of words.

Some animals live in trees.   4   5   6

A bird is in a nest.   4   5   6

2. Match the uppercase and lowercase letters.

F	a
W	f
A	t
O	w
T	o

3. Say the name of each picture. Circle the pictures whose names rhyme.

4. Say the name of each picture. Circle the number of syllables.

1 2 3   1 2 3   1 2 3   1 2 3

5. Say the name of each picture. Color only the letters whose sounds you hear in each word.

h	s	u	n

t	l	o	p

r	u	a	g

6. Read each word. Change one letter to spell the name of the picture.

zip   _____   wet   _____

Print Directionality

Color the left object in each pair.

1.

2.

3.

4.

5. Look at the pages. Follow the directions.
Circle the page on the left.
Draw a green dot where you would begin reading.
Draw a red **X** where you stop reading.
Color the picture or illustration.

Once upon a time, an old woman baked a gingerbread man. Before he was done cooking, he jumped out of the oven. The old woman, the old man, the boy, and the cat chased the gingerbread man. But, they could not catch him. Then, he came to a river where a fox tricked him. The fox gobbled him up.

Words in Print

1. Circle the words.

with 3

ball g

go B

6 you

up

can that

Circle the number of words in each sentence.

2. We read a book.   3   4   5

3. You ran fast.   3   4   5

4. Let's play a game.   3   4   5

5. She eats a red apple.   3   4   5

6. Do your best.   3   4   5

Letters

Use the uppercase and lowercase letter cards to assess students' letter recognition and letter formation. Display one card at a time and have students tell what letter is shown. Or, have students sort and then match the upper- and lowercase letters. To assess writing letters, present an upper- or lowercase letter and have students write the other form. If desired, laminate the cards for durability.

A	B	C	D
E	F	G	H
I	J	K	L
M	N	O	P

Q	R	S	T
U	V	W	X
Y	Z	a	b
c	d	e	f
g	h	i	j

k	l	m	n
o	p	q	r
s	t	u	v
w	x	y	z

Letter Recognition

Match each uppercase letter to its lowercase letter.

A	h	N	p
B	f	O	x
C	c	P	t
D	b	Q	w
E	l	R	z
F	j	S	o
G	a	T	r
H	d	U	v
I	m	V	s
J	e	W	y
K	g	X	u
L	i	Y	q
M	k	Z	n

Rhyming Words and Pictures

Use the rhyming words and picture cards to assess students' phonological awareness and recognition of rhyming words. Ask students to say the names of the pictures. Then, have them match cards whose names rhyme. Alternatively, place cards facedown. Have a student turn over a card, say the name of the picture, and produce an additional rhyming word. If desired, laminate the cards for durability.

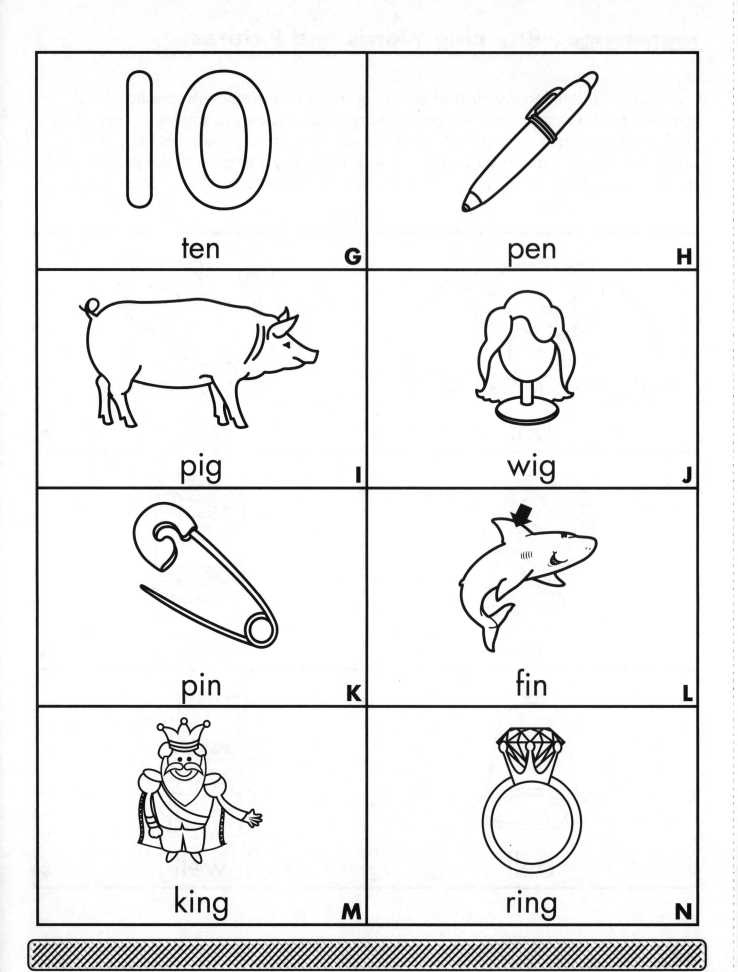

ten **G**

pen **H**

pig **I**

wig **J**

pin **K**

fin **L**

king **M**

ring **N**

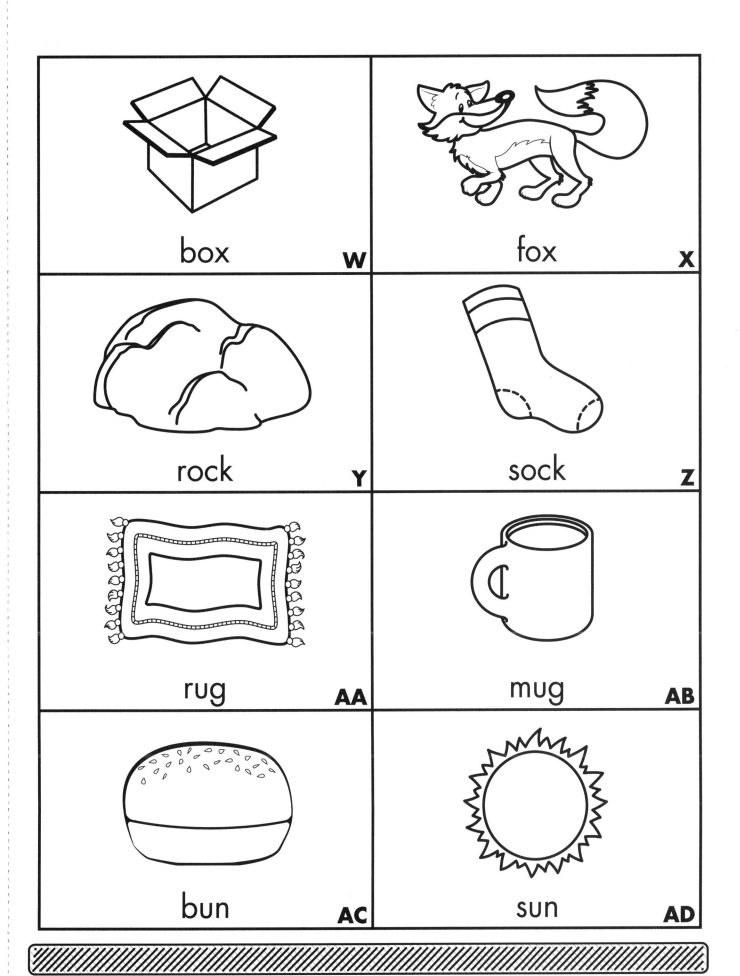

box **W**

fox **X**

rock **Y**

sock **Z**

rug **AA**

mug **AB**

bun **AC**

sun **AD**

Rhyming

Say the name of each picture. Color the two pictures in each row whose names rhyme.

1.

2.

3.

4.

5.

6.

Say the name of each picture. Draw a picture of something that rhymes.

7.

8.

9.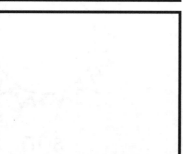

10.

Syllables

Say the name of each picture. Circle the number of syllables in the word.

1.  1 2 3	**2.**  1 2 3	**3.**  1 2 3
4.  1 2 3	**5.**  1 2 3	**6.**  1 2 3
7.  1 2 3	**8.**  1 2 3	**9.**  1 2 3

Name _____ Date _____

Making Words

Say the name of each picture. Write **-at** to complete each word.

1.  b _____   **2.**  c _____

3.  h _____   **4.**  m _____

Say the name of each picture. Write the beginning letter to complete each word.

5.   _____en   **6.**   _____en

7.   _____en   **8.** 10 _____en

Use the letters and the word parts to write six words.

| b d f h p r | | an ed ig ot ug |

9. _____   **10.** _____

11. _____   **12.** _____

13. _____   **14.** _____

Three-Letter Words

Say the name of each picture. Color the letters of the sounds you hear.

1.

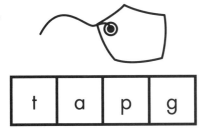

| t | a | p | g |

2.

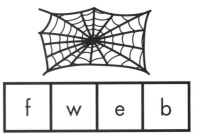

| f | w | e | b |

3.

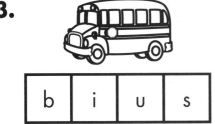

| b | i | u | s |

4.

| f | i | l | n |

5.

| h | l | o | g |

6.

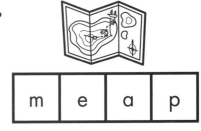

| m | e | a | p |

7.

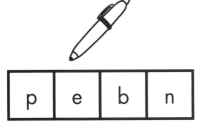

| p | e | b | n |

8.

| w | u | i | g |

9.

| c | u | p | d |

10.

| t | m | o | p |

Changing a Sound

Read each word. Change one letter to name the picture. Write the word.

1. ten _____

2. hat  _____

3. far _____

4. dot _____

5. hog _____

6. bad _____

7. pig _____

8. mat _____

9. lid _____

10. cap _____

Beginning and Ending Sounds

Say the name of each picture. Circle the letter of the beginning sound.

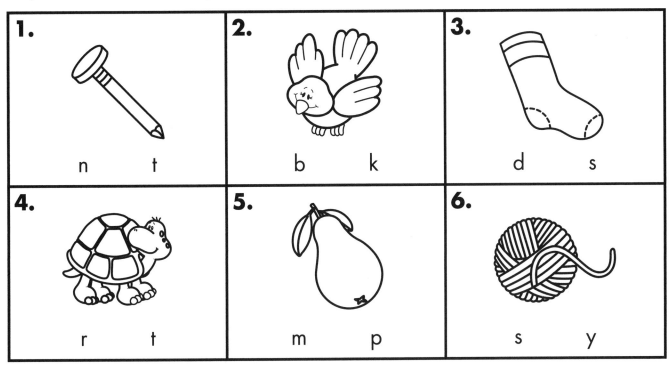

1.
n   t

2.
b   k

3.
d   s

4.
r   t

5.
m   p

6.
s   y

Say the name of each picture. Circle the letter of the ending sound.

7.
f   t

8.
l   r

9.
k   m

10.
b   f

11.
r   l

12.
p   n

Short Vowel Sounds

Circle the word that names each picture.

1.

fan

fin

2.

map

mop

3.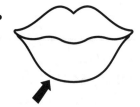

lap

lip

4.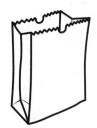

bag

bog

5.

pan

pin

6.

jog

jug

7.

tap

top

8.

bad

bed

9.

cat

cot

10.

leg

log

Word Lists

Words for Language Assessments

Use these lists of words when you are assessing language concepts. The lists are not comprehensive but can be used as grade-level examples for creating your own assessments, flash cards, etc.

Sight Words

a
all
am
and
at
big
but
can
do
for
go
had
he
here
him
his
I
in
is
it
like
little
look
my
no
on
of
said
see
she
that
the
they
to
up
was
with
yes
you

Short Vowels
Words with Short A

bag
bat
can
cap
cat
fan
hat
jam
map
mat
tag
van

Words with Short E

bed
egg
gem
hen
jet
leg
men
net
pen
red
ten
vet
web

Words with Short I

bib
dig
fin
hip
lid
lip
pig
pin
six
wig

Words with Short O

box
cob
cot
dot
fox
log
mop
top

Words with Short U

bug
bun
bus
cub
cup
hut
jug
mug
nut
pup
rug
sun
tub

One-Syllable Words

boat
car
desk
fan
frog
game
girl
gum
kite
lamp
leaf
map
nine
nose
rock
school
six
tape

Two-Syllable Words

carrot
circus
dentist
giraffe
helmet
lion
mitten
muffin
peanut
pencil
puppy
rabbit
seven
sister
spider
summer
toaster
turkey
window

Three-Syllable Words

banana
blueberry
butterfly
elephant
eleven
eraser
grasshopper
hospital
octopus
pajamas
piano
strawberry
tomato
umbrella

The Twins

Kim and Kay are twins. They like to do a lot of the same things. They both like to dance. They both like to swim. They both like to ride bikes.

But, even twins like to do different things. Kim likes to wear shorts. Kay wears skirts. Kim likes bows in her hair. Kay likes her hair down. Kim likes to wear flip-flops. Kay likes to wear sneakers.

Both girls think it is fun to have a twin.

The Twins

Kim and Kay are twins. They like to do a lot of the same   14

things. They both like to dance. They both like to swim. They   26

both like to ride bikes.   31

But, even twins like to do different things. Kim likes to   42

wear shorts. Kay wears skirts. Kim likes bows in her hair. Kay   54

likes her hair down. Kim likes to wear flip-flops. Kay likes to   66

wear sneakers.   68

Both girls think it is fun to have a twin.   78

Number of Words Read	Words per Minute	Words Read in Error
First Try		
Second Try		
Third Try		

The Fat Cat

There was a fat cat,
Who sat on a hat.
The big hat went flat.
"Meow, meow!" said the cat.

The Fat Cat

There was a fat cat,	5
Who sat on a hat.	10
The big hat went flat.	15
"Meow, meow!" said the cat.	20

Number of Words Read	Words per Minute	Words Read in Error
First Try		
Second Try		
Third Try		

Fluency Comprehension Questions

The Twins (pages 54 and 55)

1. What do both girls like to do?
2. Who likes to wear bows in her hair?
3. What does Kay wear that Kim does not like to wear?
4. How do the girls feel about being twins?

The Fat Cat (pages 56 and 57)

1. What did the cat sit on?
2. What happened to the hat?
3. What did the cat say?

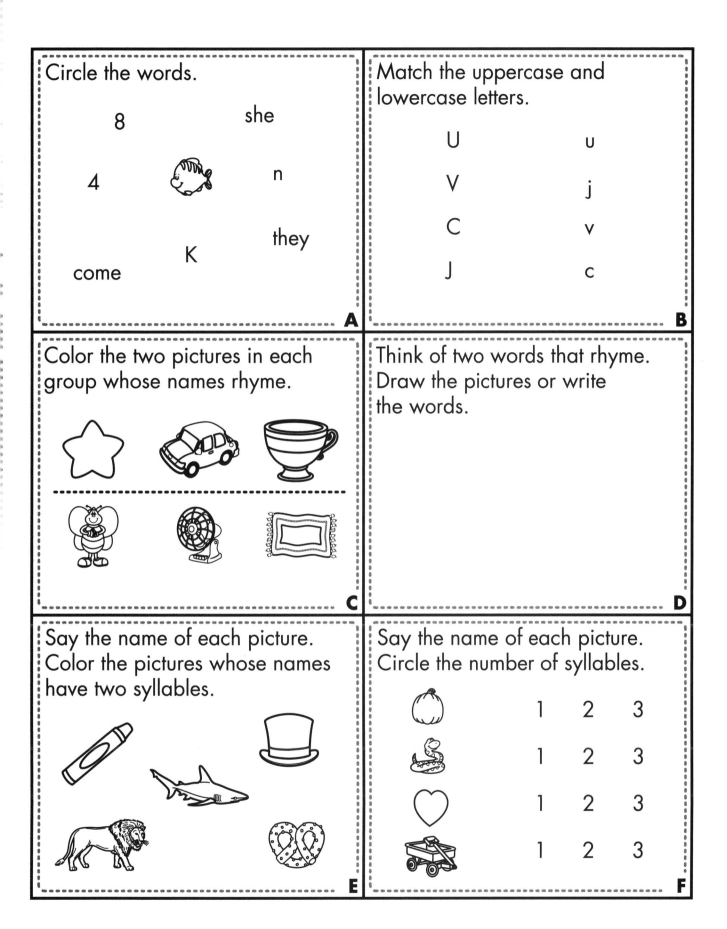

Circle the words.

8

she

4

n

they

come

K

A

Match the uppercase and lowercase letters.

U   u

V   j

C   v

J   c

B

Color the two pictures in each group whose names rhyme.

C

Think of two words that rhyme. Draw the pictures or write the words.

D

Say the name of each picture. Color the pictures whose names have two syllables.

E

Say the name of each picture. Circle the number of syllables.

1   2   3

1   2   3

1   2   3

1   2   3

F

Write the letter for each sound you hear.

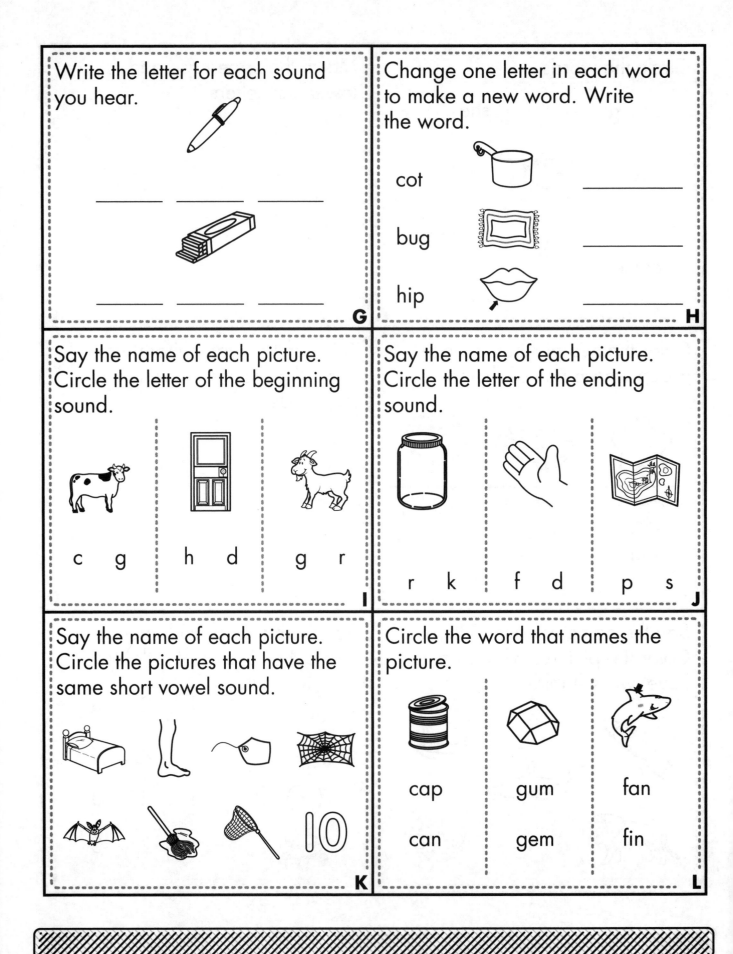

_____ _____ _____

_____ _____ _____

G

Change one letter in each word to make a new word. Write the word.

cot   _____

bug   _____

hip   _____

H

Say the name of each picture. Circle the letter of the beginning sound.

c   g   h   d   g   r

I

Say the name of each picture. Circle the letter of the ending sound.

r   k   f   d   p   s

J

Say the name of each picture. Circle the pictures that have the same short vowel sound.

K

Circle the word that names the picture.

cap   gum   fan

can   gem   fin

L

Writing an Opinion Piece

If you could be a dog or a cat, which would you be? Draw or write three reasons to support your opinion.

Writing an Explanatory Text

Draw and write about an animal.

All About _____

_____ are _____

_____

_____

_____ .

_____ can _____

_____

_____

_____ .

_____ have _____

_____

_____

_____ .

Writing a Narrative

Complete the narrative by drawing or writing.

Think about a time you learned something new. How did you learn it?

First,

Then,

Finally,

I like to eat _____.
Draw it.

A

I like to play _____.
Draw it.

B

The animal I like best is a

_____

because _____

_____

_____

_____.

C

Draw the steps to make a

_____.

D

Write a sentence to begin a story about a time you felt happy.

_____

_____

_____

_____

E

Write a sentence to begin a story about a time you felt scared.

_____

_____

_____

_____

F

✦ Show What You Know ✦
Language: Conventions

1. Write the missing letters of the alphabet.

A		C	D		F		H	I			L	M
N			Q	R			U	V	W		Y	

2. Circle the nouns. Draw an **X** on the verbs.

car   run   talk

jump

shoe   egg

3. Circle the correct word for each picture.

bibs   fox   book

bib   foxes   books

4. Circle the question word in each sentence.

When will we go?   How do you feel?

5. Look at the dot. Circle the word that tells where the dot is.

in   out   over   under

6. Circle the capital letters. Write the correct ending punctuation.

A car has four tires

Why did the dog bark

Name _____ Date _____

1. Write the missing letters of the alphabet.

	b		d		f	g		i	j		l	
	o	p		r		t				w	x		z

2. Circle the nouns. Draw an **X** on the verbs.

truck   walk   eat   sleep

toy   apple

3. Circle the correct word for each picture.

   (bees image)

cows   pens   bee

cow   pen   bees

4. Circle the question word in each sentence.

What is your name?   Who is that boy?

5. Look at the dot. Circle the word that tells where the dot is.

near   far   over   under

6. Circle the capital letters. Write the correct ending punctuation.

A bird is on the branch

How old are you

Printing Uppercase Letters

Write the uppercase letter next to each lowercase letter.

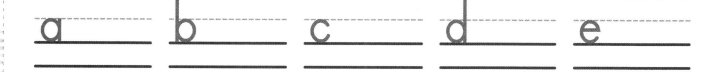

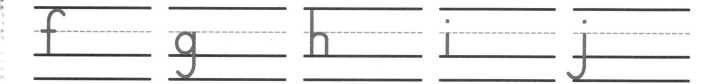

Printing Lowercase Letters

Write the lowercase letter next to each uppercase letter.

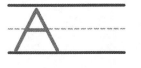 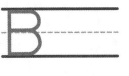 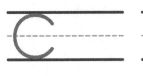 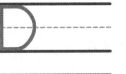 

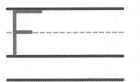    

 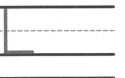  

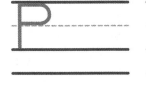 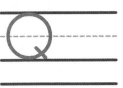  

 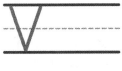 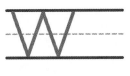

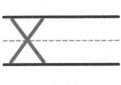 

Name _____ Date _____

Nouns

Color the stars that have nouns in them.

 bed

 baby

 tree

 sock

 hop

 ball

 bug

sing

kick

house

 book

 kite

Verbs

Color the bubbles that have verbs in them.

sleep   cut   boy

read   run   jump

girl   cat   dig

eat   play   dog

Plural Nouns

Circle the word that names each picture.

1.

hat   hats

2.

egg   eggs

3.

shoe   shoes

4.

dog   dogs

5.

rock   rocks

6.
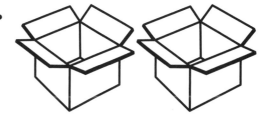
box   boxes

7.
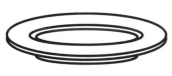
dish   dishes

8.

dress   dresses

Question Words

1. Circle the words that can begin a question.

Who	There	When
What	See	Why
How	Where	Talk

Circle the picture that could be an answer to the question.

2. What can I use to eat with?

3. When do we sleep?

4. Where can we play?

Name _____ Date _____

Prepositions

Look at the rabbit. Circle the word that tells where it is.

1.

in   on

2.

beside   above

3.

over   under

4.

in front of   on top of

5.

over   under

6.

above   behind

7.

in   on

8.

between   below

Capitalization

Circle the word or words that should be capitalized in each sentence.

1. may i have pizza?

2. my dad said that i could.

3. thank you very much.

3. pizza is my favorite food.

4. what is your favorite food?

5. i like apples too.

6. Write the words that you circled.

_____   _____

_____   _____

_____   _____

_____   _____

Ending Punctuation

Circle the ending punctuation in each sentence with the correct color.

> period = green
> question mark = yellow
> exclamation point = red

1. Watch me dive!

2. They drove to school.

3. He jumps on the rock.

4. How old are you?

5. Look out!

6. She sat next to Ella.

7. Do you have a blue bike?

8. We are going to the mall.

Write the correct ending punctuation for each sentence.

9. A bug is on a leaf

10. What is your name

Spelling

Say the name of each picture. Write the word.

1. _____ _ _ _ _ _ _ _ _ _ _____	**2.** _____ _ _ _ _ _ _ _ _ _ _____
3. _____ _ _ _ _ _ _ _ _ _ _____	**4.** _____ _ _ _ _ _ _ _ _ _ _____
5. _____ _ _ _ _ _ _ _ _ _ _____	**6.** _____ _ _ _ _ _ _ _ _ _ _____
7. _____ _ _ _ _ _ _ _ _ _ _____	**8.** _____ _ _ _ _ _ _ _ _ _ _____
9. _____ _ _ _ _ _ _ _ _ _ _____	**10.** _____ _ _ _ _ _ _ _ _ _ _____

Write the uppercase letters in order.

A

Write the lowercase letters in order.

B

Look at the picture. Read the text. Find two nouns and two verbs. Write them.

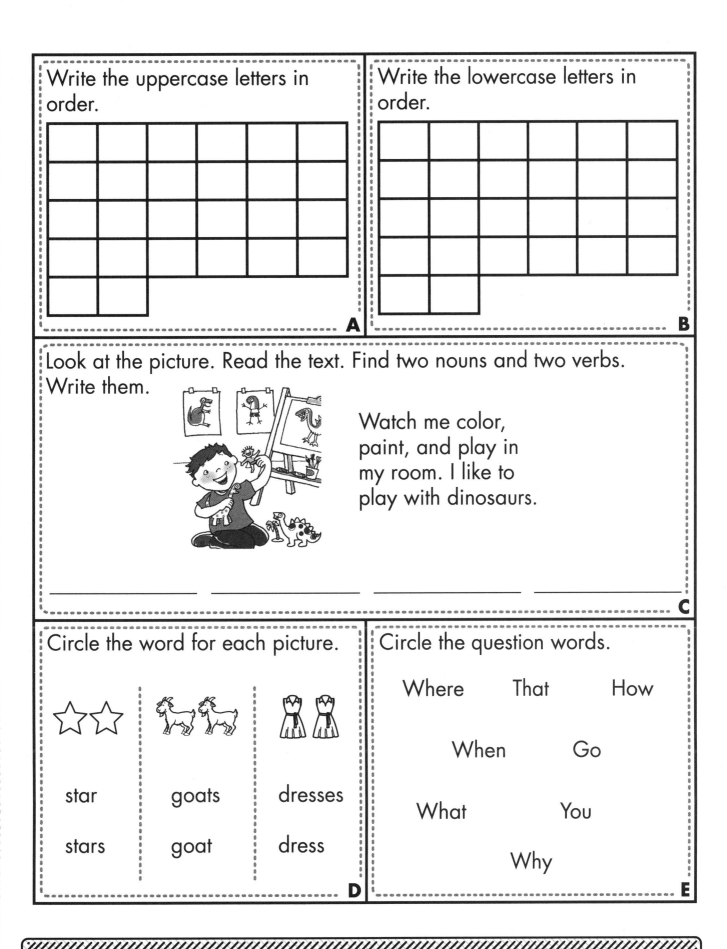

Watch me color, paint, and play in my room. I like to play with dinosaurs.

_____ _____ _____ _____

C

Circle the word for each picture.

star
stars

goats
goat

dresses
dress

D

Circle the question words.

Where   That   How

When   Go

What   You

Why

E

Draw an **X** <u>below</u> the house.
Draw a circle <u>around</u> the house.
Draw a tree <u>next to</u> the house.
Draw a bird <u>above</u> the house.

F

Rewrite the sentence. Correct the words that should be capitalized.

where are you and i going?

_____

_____

_____

G

Write the correct ending punctuation for each sentence.

I love pizza [ ]

Jesse gave me a gift [ ]

When does the plane land [ ]

H

Write the correct ending punctuation for each sentence.

When can you come over [ ]

Look out for the hole [ ]

These shoes are too tight [ ]

I

Say the name of each picture. Write the letters for the sounds you hear.

___ ___ ___

___ ___ ___

___ ___ ___

J

Say the name of each picture. Write the letters for the sounds you hear.

___ ___ ___

___ ___ ___

___ ___ ___

K

Name _____   Date _____

✦ Show What You Know ✦
Language: Vocabulary

Read each pair of sentences. Write the word that makes sense in both sentences.

(fan   bark)

1. The _____ on the tree is brown.

Listen to the big dog _____.

2. I turned on the _____ to cool off.

The _____ cheered at the game.

Write the prefix or suffix to complete each word.

(un-   re-   -ful   -less)

3. _____ tie = the opposite of tie

4. help_____ = without help

5. _____ view = view again

6. care_____ = full of care

7. Look at each group of pictures. Draw a line to name the group.

         farm animals

         fruit

8. Color each box to match the words to their opposite meanings.

on		back		wet		sad	
happy		dry		front		off	

✦ Show What You Know ✦
Language: Vocabulary

Read each pair of sentences. Write the word that makes sense in both sentences.

    ┌─────────────────┐
    │   saw   star   │
    └─────────────────┘

1. Jane was the _____ of the show.

He drew a _____ on his paper.

2. Matt _____ a lion at the zoo.

Dad cut the tree with a _____.

Write the prefix or suffix to complete each word.

    ┌──────────────────────────────┐
    │   un-   re-   -ful   -less │
    └──────────────────────────────┘

3. _____lock = the opposite of lock   **4.** hope_____ = without hope

5. _____read = read again   **6.** help_____ = full of help

7. Look at each group of pictures. Draw a line to name the group.

     zoo animals

     tools

8. Color each box to match the words to their opposite meanings.

young	hot	old	out
in	little	big	cold

Multiple-Meaning Words

Say the name of each picture. Draw a line from each word to the picture that matches the word.

ring

bat

bark

foot

Use one of the words in a sentence. Color the picture that shows the meaning.

_____

_____

_____

Name _____ Date _____

Affixes

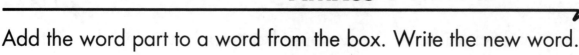

Add the word part to a word from the box. Write the new word.

1. re- + (do   play   read) = _____

2. un- + (tie   lock   fold) = _____

3. (hope   joy   wish) + -ful = _____

4. (help   fear   care) + -less = _____

5. Choose one of the words from above. Write a sentence or draw a picture to show the word's meaning.

Sorting Words by Category

Draw a line to match each object to the correct category.

toys

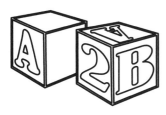

clothes

Opposites

Circle the two pictures in each row whose names are antonyms, or opposites.

1.

up   left   down

2.

cold   hot   stop

3.

day   night   old

4.

hard   hot   soft

5.

slow   sharp   fast

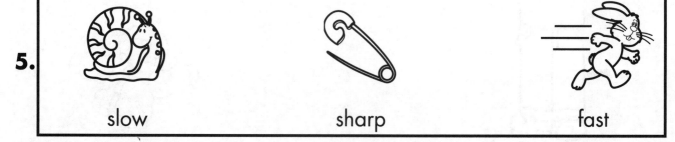

Adjectives

Look at the pictures. Use a **blue** crayon to circle the objects that are **soft**. Use a **red** crayon to circle the objects that can be **hot**. Use a **yellow** crayon to circle the objects that can be **hard**.

bathtub	bed	stove	toothbrush
table	soap	cup	pillow
comb	lamp	towel	spoon
plate	fork	pan	hair dryer

Shades of Meaning

Circle the words that describe the action in each picture. Choose one word to complete each sentence.

1.

cleans

washes

scrubs

walks

feeds

The boy _____ his dog.

2.

moves

calls

dances

boogies

talks

The boy _____ to the music.

Word Lists

Words for Language Assessments

Use these lists of words when you are assessing language concepts. The lists are not comprehensive but can be used as grade-level examples for creating your own assessments, flash cards, etc.

Homonyms

back
bank
bark
bat
bear
bill
book
bug
can
club
duck
fair
fire
fly
game
goal
hand
jam
kid
leaf
mouse
park
pen
plant
rock
ruler
scale
suit
train
trip
watch
wave

Affixes

un-

unable
uncover
undo
undress
uneven
unfair
unhappy
unlike
unlock
unwrap
untrue

re-

redo
refill
reheat
reload
remove
rename
repack
reread
rerun
retell
rewrite

pre-

precook
prepay
preschool
preview

-ful

careful
cheerful
colorful
fearful
helpful
hopeful
joyful
painful
playful
thankful
useful
wonderful

-less

careless
fearless
harmless
homeless
hopeless
painless
restless
sleepless
useless
worthless

Word Lists

Antonyms

above/below
big/little
buy/sell
empty/full
first/last
front/back
give/take
happy/sad
hard/soft
high/low
in/out
left/right
loud/quiet
night/day
old/new
stop/go
tall/short
wet/dry
win/lose

Synonyms/Shades of Meaning

run/jog/race/sprint
walk/stroll/strut/hike
look/stare/watch/gaze
said/stated/shouted/whispered
laugh/chuckle/giggle/snicker

Categories

Shapes

circle
rectangle
square
triangle

Sports

baseball
basketball
bowling
football
soccer

Desserts

cake
candy
cookies
ice cream

School Tools

crayons
glue
pencils
scissors
markers

Write the word that fits in both sentences.

James shut the _____ door.

Tara swam on her _____ .

A

Write the word that fits in both sentences.

I ate a buttered _____ with dinner.

Sam will _____ the ball to her.

B

Use the affix to help you write the meaning of **unhappy**.

_____

_____

_____

C

Use the affix to help you write the meaning of **reuse**.

_____

_____

_____

D

Use the affix to help you write the meaning of **fearless**.

_____

_____

_____

E

Use the affix to help you write the meaning of **helpful**.

_____

_____

_____

F

Write the name for each category.

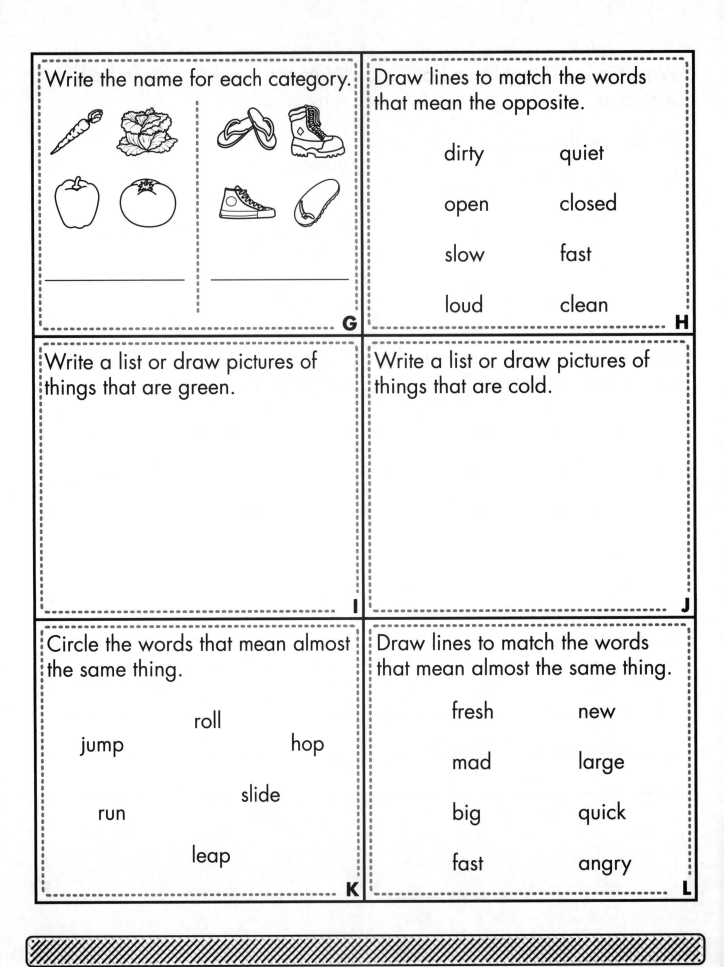

_____   _____

G

Draw lines to match the words that mean the opposite.

dirty   quiet

open   closed

slow   fast

loud   clean

H

Write a list or draw pictures of things that are green.

I

Write a list or draw pictures of things that are cold.

J

Circle the words that mean almost the same thing.

roll

jump   hop

slide

run

leap

K

Draw lines to match the words that mean almost the same thing.

fresh   new

mad   large

big   quick

fast   angry

L

Answer Key

Page 9
1. friends; 2. special; 3. happy; 4. bus

Page 10
1. boy; 2. sleeping; 3. picture; 4. poem

Page 11
1. Andy, Mom; 2. store; 3. excited;
4. snack

Page 12
Answers will vary.

Page 15
1. pond; 2. boy, man; 3. It was a sunny day. The boy caught a big fish.

Page 16
1. poem; 2. story; 3. Answers will vary.

Page 17
1. C; 2. B; 3. A

Page 18
Goldilocks and the Three Bears: curious, sleepy, three bears, porridge, chair; Both: little girl, woods, bed; *Little Red Riding Hood*: brave, helpful, wolf, basket, Grandma

Pages 19–20
A–E. Check students' work. F. Answers will vary but could include a beach or pool setting. G. Check students' work. H. Answers will vary but should show the snowman getting taller or more complete. I–J. Check students' work. K. crayons, pencils; L. Check students' work.

Page 21
1. picture; 2. text; 3. hunt; 4. hunted too much; 5. to teach you about tigers

Page 22
1. a cold-blooded animal; 2. scales; 3. square, diamond; 4. rain forests; 5. so that you can see the scales

Page 23
1. in forests; 2. black and white; 3. bamboo; 4. trees

Page 24
1. Animals have homes. 2. trees; 3. ground; 4. caves

Page 25
1. same; 2. different; 3. same; 4. different; 5. same; 6. same; 7. different; 8. Check students' work.

Answer Key

Page 26
1. skin; 2. flesh; 3–4. Check students' work.

Page 27
Check students' work.

Page 28
Check students' work.

Page 29
1–2. Check students' work. 3. writes words; 4. draws pictures

Page 30
Check students' work.

Page 31
1. Kit; 2. her cat is lost; 3. missing; 4. riddle; 5. to entertain you

Page 32
1–4. Check students' work.

Pages 33–34
A–F. Check students' work. G. title page; H. Check students' work. I. It helps you understand what the words mean. J. Check students' work. K. to show you; L. Check students' work.

Page 35
1. 6, 4; 2. Check students' work. 3. hat, bat, cat; 4. 2, 1, 1, 2; 5. web, can, pig; 6. hen, fan

Page 36
1. 5, 6; 2. Check students' work. 3. pen, ten, hen; 4. 1, 3, 1, 2; 5. sun, top, rug; 6. lip, net

Page 37
1–5. Check students' work.

Page 38
1. The following words should be circled: go, up, can, you, ball, that, with. 2. 4; 3. 3; 4. 4; 5. 5; 6. 3

Page 42
Check students' work.

Page 46
1. mop, top; 2. log, dog; 3. pig, wig; 4. bag, flag; 5. bat, hat; 6. man, can; 7–10. Check students' work.

Page 47
1. 2; 2. 3; 3. 1; 4. 3; 5. 3; 6. 1; 7. 1; 8. 2; 9. 2

Answer Key

Page 48

1. bat; 2. cat; 3. hat; 4. mat; 5. hen; 6. men; 7. pen; 8. ten; 9–14. Answers will vary.

Page 49

1. tag; 2. web; 3. bus; 4. fin; 5. log; 6. map; 7. pen; 8. wig; 9. cup; 10. mop

Page 50

1. hen; 2. bat; 3. car; 4. pot; 5. dog; 6. bag; 7. pin; 8. map; 9. lip; 10. can

Page 51

1. n; 2. b; 3. s; 4. t; 5. p; 6. y; 7. t; 8. l; 9. m; 10. f; 11. r; 12. n

Page 52

1. fan; 2. mop; 3. lip; 4. bag; 5. pin; 6. jug; 7. top; 8. bed; 9. cat; 10. log

Page 58

The Twins: 1. Answers will vary but may include, dance, swim, or ride bikes. 2. Kim; 3. Answers will vary but may include skirts or sneakers. 4. The girls think that it is fun to be twins. *The Fat Cat*: 1. hat; 2. It went flat. 3. "Meow, meow!"

Pages 59–60

A. come, she, they; B. Uu, Vv, Cc, Jj; C. star and car, bug and rug; D. Check students' work. E. crayon, lion, pretzel; F. 2, 1, 1, 2; G. pen, gum; H. pot, rug, lip; I. c, d, g; J. r, d, p; K. bed, leg, web, net, ten; L. can, gem, fin

Page 61

Answers will vary.

Page 62

Answers will vary.

Page 63

Answers will vary.

Page 64

A–F. Check students' work.

Page 65

1. B, E, G, J, K, O, P, S, T, X, Z; 2. nouns: car, shoe, egg; verbs: jump, run, talk; 3. bibs, foxes, books; 4. When, How; 5. in, over; 6. A, W, ., ?

Page 66

1. a, c, e, h, k, m, n, q, s, u, v, y; 2. nouns: truck, toy, apple; verbs: walk, eat, sleep; 3. cows, pens, bees; 4. What, Who; 5. near, under; 6. A, H, ., ?

Answer Key

Page 67
Check students' work.

Page 68
Check students' work.

Page 69
bed, sock, baby, tree, bug, ball, house, book, kite

Page 70
sleep, cut, read, run, jump, dig, eat, play

Page 71
1. hats; 2. eggs; 3. shoes; 4. dog;
5. rock; 6. boxes; 7. dish; 8. dresses

Page 72
1. Who, When, What, Why, How, Where; 2. spoon; 3. nighttime moon;
4. playground

Page 73
1. on; 2. beside; 3. under; 4. in front of;
5. over; 6. behind; 7. in; 8. between

Page 74
1. May, I; 2. My, I; 3. Thank; 4. Pizza;
5. I; 6. See 1–5.

Page 75
1. red; 2. green; 3. green; 4. yellow;
5. red; 6. green; 7. yellow; 8. green;
9. .; 10. ?

Page 76
1. can; 2. pin; 3. tub; 4. cap; 5. pan;
6. net; 7. bag; 8. gum; 9. bib; 10. mop

Pages 77–78
A–B. Check students' work. C. Answers will vary. D. stars, goats, dresses;
E. Where, How, When, What, Why;
F. Check students' work. G. Where are you and I going? H. !, ., ?; I. ?, !, .;
J. net, hat, bus; K. jam, lip, top

Page 79
1. bark; 2. fan; 3. un-; 4. -less; 5. re-;
6. -ful; 7. farm animals: cow, horse, pig, duck; fruit: apple, pear, grapes, cherries;
8. front/back, wet/dry, happy/sad, on/off

Page 80
1. star; 2. saw; 3. un-; 4. -less; 5. re-;
6. -ful; 7. zoo animals: zebra, lion, tiger, bear; tools: saw, hammer, drill, shovel;
8. young/old, hot/cold, big/little, in/out;

Page 81
Check students' work.

Answer Key

Page 82

Answers will vary.

Page 83

Toys: teddy bear, blocks, truck, doll;
Clothes: shirt, shoe, pants, hat,
sock, coat

Page 84

1. up, down; 2. cold, hot; 3. day, night;
4. hard, soft; 5. slow, fast

Page 85

Answers will vary.

Page 86

1. cleans, washes, scrubs; 2. moves,
dances, boogies

Pages 89–90

A. back; B. roll; C. opposite of happy;
D. use again; E. without fear; F. full of
help; G. vegetables, shoes; H. dirty/
clean, open/closed, slow/fast, loud/
quiet; I–J. Answers will vary. K. jump,
hop, leap; L. fresh/new, mad/angry,
big/large, fast/quick

Notes